THE WEALTH OF AN INTERCESSOR

SABRINA SMITH

The Wealth of An Intercessor

@Copyright © 2022 by Sabrina Smith

ISBN: 978-1-953638-36-6

LCCN: 2022900970

Printed in the United States of America

PUBLISHER

TA MEDIA & PRODUCTIONS LLC

DALLAS, TX 75240

www.PUBLISHYOURBOOKTODAY.INFO

WWW.TAMEDIACO.COM

Unless otherwise noted, all Scripture quotations are taken from the Holy Bible, King James Version

(PUBLIC DOMAIN PER BIBLEGATEWAY.COM)

Holy Bible, New International Version®, NIV® Copyright ©1973, 1978, 1984, 2011 by Biblica, Inc.® Used by permission. All rights reserved worldwide.

The Holy Bible, English Standard Version. ESV® Text Edition: 2016. Copyright © 2001 by Crossway Bibles, a publishing ministry of Good News Publishers.

TABLE OF CONTENTS

INTRODUCTION

I feel so honor that God would entrust me to write this book. I was challenged in my mind wondering if I was qualified to write such book like this, being that when I look at my own life, it did not match the title of this book. However, we tend to have only one-dimensional thought of what wealth and prosperity is and what it looks like. A lot of it is adopted from a worldly perspective, such as a big house, designer clothing and multiple cars. In other words, having an abundance of materials and assets. Do not get me wrong, having those things are fine, but it is not the totality of living an abundant life and living in the fullness of God. Many times, we have yielded to the place of prayer and intercession and have left that space still broken in the natural and spiritual. We may have experienced some victories and increases yet it was not sustainable, and we found ourselves in lack again. What does that mean? It means, we have found ourselves in cycles that did not produce abundance. An abundance of joy, peace, prosperity, wealth, good health, sound mind and changed mindset.

In preparing to write, I pondered on many things, one of which is why I was struggling to write, and I kept coming back to this one thought. God reminded me, I prophesied to you concerning wealth, I have spoken through my prophets to you, and I have broken the curse of poverty in your bloodline. When God brought that to my remembrance, it gave me the courage to trust Him and write. It also let me know, He has given me the authority to write this book. He gave me the title and content, however for the life of me, I did not understand it at first. I soon realized this has been assigned and ordained for me to release this content by way of revelation from Him. I struggled for a while, but He freed me from the opinions of others and as well as my own opinion of myself as it relates to being qualified. I almost disqualified myself from this awesome opportunity and assignment. All I needed to do was walk it out in obedience, while leaning into Gods' heart. To tell you the truth, there were days where I would sit with my laptop and not hear anything, I almost felt like I was in error. However, I soon learned I needed to discipline myself, cast down unfruitful thoughts and continuously surrender my heart to God. I really felt like God was setting me up. I sensed that a divine impartation would take place as I sought His heart. Some of you will experience healing and restoration in your souls. Your identity will be restored, poverty will be broken, changed mindsets will take place and you'll begin to see yourself the way God sees you on another level and dimension. You see, my fellow intercessors, God has spoken wealth in and over your life, in fact, it has already been seeded within you before the foundation of the earth, Gods' purpose will prevail in your life beloved. Those of you that are called to the Marketplace and have an entrepreneurship spirit are called to this, you are called to wealth, you are called to be a financier of the Kingdom of God. You have been called to walk in your wealthy place. Some of you are so gifted and creative with your mind and hands. I encourage you to obey God and the principles of the Kingdom of God, even as it relates to integrity and stewardship. God is aligning His prophetic vessels in the seven mountains to dominate. Prayer, intercession, worship, praise, faith and taking action is required of you, remember, faith without works is dead. Romans 10:17 MSG, Faith, then is birthed in a heart that responds to Gods' anointed utterance of the Anointed One.

Trust God to give you the blueprint and strategy. There are gifts and talents inside each of you and they will continue to remain undiscovered or covered up if you do not embrace prayer and intercession as part of the plan to emerge as one that is called to walk in your wealthy place. The original seed of wealth is in the word of God. Intercessors are people of the word and doers of the word. It is time to restore the Altar of Prayer.

Meditate and speak this over your life Ecclesiastes 3:11AMP

He has made everything beautiful and appropriate in its time. He has also planted eternity [a sense of divine purpose] in the human heart [a mysterious longing which nothing under the sun can satisfy, except God]—yet man cannot find out (comprehend, grasp) what God has done (His overall plan) from the beginning to the end.

Ask God to unveil his purpose and divine will concerning your life which includes wealth and prosperity. Remember, as you take this journey, meditate on Proverbs 3:5-6

1. Trust God with all your heart.

(Trust) in the Hebrew language is Batah, meaning confidence, secure, to be bold. It is time to be bold in your trusting God. Trusting Him in this next phase of your life, next level, this place of upgrade.

2. Lean not to your own understanding

(Lean) in the Hebrew language is Sa an, meaning to rely, to lean on, to trust in, support. It is time that you begin to lean into God, His wisdom, his way of doing and thinking. This also means leaving mindsets of mediocrity and lack. You will need to feed your mind by meditation on wealth and prosperity.

3. Acknowledge God.

(Acknowledge) in the Hebrew language is Yada, this means to perceive, to consider, to declare, understand to know, to be acquainted with. In other words, you must recognize God in all that you are doing because it is not in your own strength or knowledge. It also shows your dependence on God. As God elevate you and promote you, you must be very careful to watch that pride do not arise in you. If it does, you have authority to pull it down and walk in humility. The bible tells us to be clothed in humility.

God promises to direct your path. What this means is that God will make straight your path, it will be leveled and smooth for you. So, continue to trust Him, lean not to your own understanding, and acknowledge Him.

Please read on that you may gain the wisdom, knowledge and understanding as God unfolds the revelation of the wealth of an intercessor. I'm so excited that you are receiving this impartation to walk into your wealthy place and never return to lack and poverty. You have been chosen out of your bloodline to break the curse and to produce generational wealth and prosperity.

Prayer:

Father God, I thank you for the reader of this book. I thank you that you are opening the eyes of their understanding and you will flood their hearts and minds with revelation of what you have planned for them before the foundation of the earth. I pray that their identities are restored, souls are healed, and they have emerged from fear and bloodline curses. I pray that they have now been ushered them into bloodline blessings. I pray that everything that tried to block the wealthy place of the intercessor, is now broken, and destroyed by the fire of God, in Jesus' Name, Amen.

Time of Reflection

CHAPTER 1

WEALTH AND PROSPERITY

The ultimate source of wealth and prosperity comes from God. The sacred places that an intercessor hold gives unique and monumental access. In intercession we remind God of His promises of provision and wholeness for those we have been called to as well as ourselves. Wealth and Prosperity goes beyond riches and pierces the inner man and breaks cycles. We can navigate in the spirit and identify the root cause of any hindrance or stagnation. We can go before the Father and unlock resources through prayer as well as warfare through the authority given by Jesus Christ our Lord. God has always desired for His people to live a prosperous life naturally, spiritually, and financially. He has also equipped us to manifest it. In *3 John 1:2 it says Beloved, I wish above all things that thou mayest prosper and be in health, even as thy soul prospereth. Apostle Paul was interceding for Gauis, a co-laborer in the faith whose life in the spirit was prospering but his health was not at an optimal level.*

He prayed for alignment for him because of His faithfulness to God and the work he had done for Christ. As intercessors we do the same thing today. We intercede for the whole man: saved and unsaved and God responds. He gives us wisdom to share with some we intercede for or we simply to lay it at His feet. We see His hand and heart for others, and we stay in position and complete each assignment given to us. What a privilege it is to unlock these intimate places in the Heavens that gives us access to the heart of the Father.

Although we have been given the ability to unlock prosperity and wealth for others, we must remember we have it for ourselves as well. At times we forget about ourselves, but the same power that works on the behalf of others works for us. Sometimes we need a reminder. We must also remember that God is our shield and our exceeding great reward. We are so used to going in for others, but we never come out with spoils for ourselves.

Intercessors have a unique perspective as it relates to wealth and prosperity. Our stance encompasses agreeing with the trajectory of Gods' will for our lives which then becomes the byproduct of intimacy with Him. What does this mean? The life of an intercessor is extremely distinct, and their hearts weigh differently on their perspective of wealth. While prosperity to many may be the idea of wealth as it relates to capital as this is a rather shallow view for them so to speak. It is when we truly delve into the heart and mind of God, prosperity takes on a new meaning. We manage moments, we blossom pressing towards our high calling, we thrive in uncanny situations, and we become relentless in our pursuit of Him. Every part of our lives should prosper i.e., the soul, prospering socially, economically, financially, and spiritually. Each facet becomes the systematic ecosystem that allows us to see prosperity through the lens of the Father. These areas require maturity, time, growth, discipline, and they are all intertwined with purpose. If I can be transparent, in the past I would say " if I am supposed to be prosperous, why is it taking so long"? " We would equate not having our needs met to the absence of prosperity. So being successful is prosperity maintained in every area of our lives.

Prosperity and wealth can go hand in hand, although there is a slight difference between the two. Wealth refers to the state of being rich or having an abundance of material asset and money.

Prosperity refers to being marked by success or economic well, enjoying vigorous and healthy growth by also flourishing.

As Gods intercessors, we have been given the ability to unlock both realms, however we are

required to have the mindset and heart of God concerning wealth and prosperity.

As stated, the wealth of an intercessor speaks about the spiritual inheritance and access as intercessors has to the spiritual dimension in God through the spirit. Intercessors have been granted grace to obtain this overtime through diligence, discipline, and obedience to the spirit of intercession.

This book is called to reveal what the wealth of an intercessor truly means. Intercessors stand in the gap and pray on behalf of Gods' people. We must learn that as we go in for war, we can come out with spoils. There is a seed of wealth rooted in intercessors. Let this book walk you through the journey of learning, living and manifesting what it really means to live in the wealthy place. Please understand that wealth is about covenant, covenant with God. Wealth is flowing to you and through you, establishing your covenant in the earth through divine wealth. *Deuteronomy 8:18 NIV* tells us, but remember the Lord your God, for it is He who gives you the ability to produce wealth and so confirm His covenant, which he swore to your ancestors, as it is today. This is a divine inheritance to the believers, the intercessors.

Prayer:

Father God, I pray that you are watching over your word to perform it concerning your intercessor. I pray that you will begin to cause divine alignment to take place in their lives. I break and destroy by the fire of God every sabotaging spirit that would try to infiltrate the intercessor receiving their inheritance in you. May the blood of Jesus cover their destinies as they walk in their wealthy place. Every set back that they have experienced up until now is being redeemed. Every opportunity that was missed concerning wealth and prosperity has now been restored. Father cover the seed of wealth with your intercessor by the blood of Jesus. Unlock gifts and talents within your intercessor. I pray that the anointing and grace of gaining wealth is upon them now, in Jesus' Name, Amen.

Time of Reflection:

CHAPTER 2

WHAT IS INTERCESSION:

I ntercession is intervening on another's behalf by interposing oneself between two parties and their difficulties or crisis. The Hebrew word PAGA (Strong's Hebrew #6293) is usually translated intercession and means a meeting with an outcome. It is an urging to pray given by the Holy Spirit for situations and circumstances. Intercessors are mediators that stand in the gap. Intercession is best led by the Holy Spirit. So often we do not know how to pray but the Holy Spirit is the one who helps us.

Romans 8:26 NIV, In the same way, the Spirit helps us in our weakness. We do not know what we ought to pray for, but the spirit himself intercedes for us through wordless groans.

Intercession is an invitation to relationship with God, where we understand that God wants us to use the authority and privileges we have as children of God to see the works of the enemy destroyed on earth.

God desires to partner with us to see the lives of His people redeemed, delivered, restored, and set free from lack, poverty, sickness, and disease. Prayer and intercession must be the first steps in seeing this manifest in the lives of Gods' people.

Unless the spiritual realm is first aligned, then the physical realm cannot follow. Prayer must proceed action for the action to be effective, just as sending troops in at a ground level is ineffective unless the battle for the air has first been won.

Ezekiel 22:30

And I sought for a man among them, that should make up a hedge, and stand in the gap before me for the land, that I should not destroy it, but I found none.

Sought in the Hebrew language is Baqas H1245, it means to seek, require, seek out, to secure, to seek the face and to exact. The Father is looking for those who are willing to secure their place in prayer and intercession on behalf of the land. Not only will you secure this place, but you will occupy that place of prayer and intercession and not be moved by internal or external circumstances.

Hedge in the Hebrew is Gader H1447, it means a wall or a fence. Intercessors are literally building a fence of protection through prayer and intercession. This spiritual fence is fortified against the attack of the enemy, may it be of your family, friends, community, city, or nations.

Stand in the Hebrew is Amad H5975, and it means to stand, to remain, endure, having a standing attitude, abide, persist, be steadfast and established. It is very important and key to be mentally and emotionally stable. Intercessors struggle with this a lot. The cares of life comes and beat at the hearts, minds, and emotions of intercessors. However, God has given us weapons of war, and yes intercessors get tired and weary. You must be reminded that God watches over his word to perform it concerning you, He is a promise keeper, so He won't allow you to stay in a stuck place, but you must agree with the promises of God and open your mouth despite how you feel. The Father is here to strengthen you, heal you, deliver you, and set you free from the grip of the enemy.

Gap in the Hebrew is Peres H6556, it means to breach of a wall, broken wall, outburst. This is the time where intercessors must guard their post and stand in the gap. The enemy uses breaches (walls that are broken down) in marriages, families, relationships, communities, and nations to cause even more confusion and chaos. It is because there is no unity, and the enemy has the legal right to come in.

I remember giving words of empowerment at church years ago, speaking about the benefits of a praying church. I said that it promotes unity. *Psalm 133:1 NIV*, "how good and pleasant it is when Gods' people live together in harmony." When that is broken, the enemy wreaks havoc. But in the latter verse, the bible declares the Lord bestows His blessing, even life forevermore. When we stand in the gap in unity with God and other believers in prayer and intercession, it will cease the attack of the enemy and God will also bestow His blessing to us.

Romans 8:26

Likewise, the Spirit also helpeth our infirmities, for we know not what we should pray for as we ought, but the Spirit itself maketh intercession for us with groanings which cannot be uttered. The intercessor has help in prayer and intercessions. We have heavens backing as we stand in the gap. I wanted to lay the foundation concerning intercession before we move forward.

Wealth:

Wealth is a great quantity or store of money, valuable possessions, property, or other riches. An abundance or profusion of anything, plentiful amount, the state of being rich, prosperity, affluence.

14

Deuteronomy 8:18

But thou shalt remember the Lord thy God for it is he that giveth the power to get wealth, that he may establish his covenant which he swears unto thy fathers, as it is this day.

Prosperity:

A successful, flourishing, or thriving condition, especially in financial respects, good fortune.

3 John 1:2

Beloved, I wish above all things that thou mayest prosper and be in health, even as thy soul prospereth.

Prayer:

Father God in the name of Jesus, I pray for the reader, the intercessor, your son/daughter that is reading this book, I pray for you, I pray your hearts are open and ready to receive the manifold wisdom of God. I pray that you are strengthened, revived, rejuvenated in your souls (heart, mind, and emotions). I pray that the spirit of your minds is strengthen. I pray that the eyes of your understanding be enlightened as you receive revelation of the wealth of an intercessor. I break and destroy the limitations, restraints and barriers that the enemy has tried to set against you, Gods' intercessor, I bind the spirits of lack, poverty, hardship, scarcity, deficiency, dearth, impoverishment, and destitution from off your life and I loose wealth, a wealthy mindset, affluence, riches, substance, treasure, capital, assets, finances, prosperity, abundance, resources, funds, property, and stewardship. I decree that you are flourishing and that Shalom is your portion, nothing missing, broken or lacking. I prophesy that as you read this book, you are arising to a new level of thinking, abundant thinking because you have the mind of Christ. Jesus thought it not robbery to be equal with God, may you remember that you been made in the image and likeness of God. Be reminded that you are seated in heavenly places in Christ Jesus. I pray that you begin to change your speech and change your habits that has kept you in prison of debt and cycles of poverty. I break and destroy its' power over your life by the fire of God! Burn by the fire of God, never to resurface again in and I speak wholeness to you in every area of life, may the joy of the Lord be your strength.

I activate new realms of wealth, prosperity and abundance in your life. Repeat after me, I am wealthy, I have a wealthy mindset and I am a carrier of wealth and it manifest in every area of my life.

In Jesus' Name, Amen.

Time of Reflection:

CHAPTER 3

TREASURES OF DARKNESS

Isaiah 45:1-3 Voice

This is what the Eternal One says to His chosen agent, Cyrus the Persian.

Eternal One: *Not by his hand alone, but with his in Mine, nations are vanquished, their leaders conquered; Doors and gates open without a fight and will not close. (to Cyrus) I will go ahead of you and smooth the way, lower the heights, break down bronze doors, and cut through iron bars. I will give you hidden treasures and wealth tucked away in secret places; I will reveal them to you. Then you will know that I am the Eternal, the God of Israel, who calls you by name.*

I believe we are in a crucial season of our lives and that these times require more than what we have been doing previously. Considering what's going on in the world, God is still faithful to His people. The dark times we are in, God promises that we shall not be ashamed in the evil time and in the days of famine we shall be satisfied *Psalm 37:19 KJV*. Beloved, understand that this is the hour where sacrifice is needed, and more is required of you. To enter this space where God is literally saying I will give you the hidden treasures and wealth tucked away. He is saying he will reveal them to you. This is in alignment to *Deuteronomy 8:18, But thou shalt remember the Lord thy God, for it is he that giveth thee power to get wealth, that he may establish his*

18

covenant. In both scriptures, God is letting us know that we may know He is the source of wealth. When we look at Isaiah 45:3, He is addressing Cyrus, the Persian King whom God calls His anointed. This is an appropriate title for the heathen king for two reasons, Cyrus as a temporal deliverer of God's people and serves as an illustration of Jesus Christ, the eternal redeemer and because vassal rulers were anointed by their superior rulers, Cyrus, was one who carried out God's purposes, could properly be said to be an anointed vassal. Like Jesus Christ, Cyrus' mission was to deliver and to judge. On the night the Persians captured Babylon, some of the men entered on the dry riverbed and opened the gates to their armies from the inside.

In God's purpose for Cyrus, He promised to clear the impediments to his progress and purpose. Then the promise is given in verse 3 that as Israel's God, the Lord would give Cyrus possession of the treasures of darkness. This referred to the wealth of the vanquished pagan nations which was customarily concealed in subterranean vaults. Thus, they are called the treasures of darkness and called the hidden riches of secret places because of their location. Isaiah wrote this prophecy almost 200 years before the Persian King Cyrus was born. What is so awesome about Isaiah's prophecy is its specificity. Isaiah predicted, two centuries in advance, that the coming King would be named Cyrus. He foresaw Cyrus invading Babylon and liberating the Jews from their 70-year captivity and then repatriating them to their homeland in Israel. Daniel was among the Jewish exiles that lived during the Babylonian captivity (Daniel 9). Daniel was also a student of the word and studied the scroll of Jeremiah and realized that Israel's 70 years of Babylon captivity were completed. During his study, he also discovered the name of the King that would liberate the Israelites from Babylon. It would be a Persian king named Cyrus. Soon Daniel took the scroll of Isaiah and showed him that God had recorded his name in scripture about two centuries earlier. Daniel unveiled the prophecy, it gave Cyrus the confidence to liberate the Jews from their exiles, return them to the land of Israel and announce the rebuilding of Solomon's Temple. I love this story, because it depicts God's sovereignty and faithfulness of His plan and purpose for humanity. There's something more to notice. God would not let Cyrus liberate Israel without recompense. The Lord said: Cyrus, when you free Israel and accomplish my purpose, I will give you the treasures of darkness and wealth stored in secret places. Once Cyrus freed the Jews, he also granted them permission to rebuild their Temple. In fact, Cyrus issued an edict (official decree) for them to rebuild their temple in Jerusalem and when King Cyrus did that, his soldiers back in Babylon unearthed vast amounts of silver, and gold, including the Jewish Temple treasures that was had hidden under the Euphrates River (underground vault). God's word through Isaiah had been fulfilled to the letter when He said, "I will give you treasures of darkness and wealth stored in secret places' '. God wanted Cyrus to know that He had given it to him, and Cyrus decreed the stolen items to be returned to Solomon's Temple. Cyrus's decree provided all the wealth and resources needed to rebuild the temple and the walls of Jerusalem. What has been stolen was restored. This is the same plan God has for you. You are His Anointed, whom He calls by name. No longer allow the enemy to make you feel like you do not fit into the plan of God concerning wealth. Do you see how God wants us claiming His blessings? As Cyrus illustrates, they are claimed by acting in faith. No one will receive the treasures of darkness or wealth stored in secret places without acting in faith. You must move toward the plan that God has ordained for your life.

Beloved Intercessor, God wants to open your eyes to things that would otherwise remain unseen, so you can claim what would otherwise remain unclaimed. The treasures of darkness are stored in all places' darkness and wealth of secret places, hidden in all locations, secret places. That means these treasures surround us and the good news is this: God is not trying to hide treasures from us, He is hiding them for us as you see with King Cyrus. Here's the last part to this because we can ask ourselves, why does God want to give us the treasures of darkness? Remember the Lord said to Cyrus in *Isaiah 45:3*, I'm doing all this so you will know it is I, the God of Israel that calls you by name. You must know nothing God does is without purpose and His purpose for recompensing Cyrus was to reveal himself as the true and living God. The Lord wanted this Persian King convinced that the God of Abraham, Isaac, and Jacob was the Sovereign Lord of creation. God certifies His sovereignty by calling Cyrus by name two centuries before his birth and then predicting that Cyrus will collect the treasures of darkness. God has a similar message for you. God has spoken to you through his word, His prophets, he has also given you dreams. God is saying to you beloved; I foreknew you long before your birth, even before the foundation of the earth. The Lord wants to reveal Himself and reward you as you follow His divine plan. I remember years ago, when I worked for a company in the Call Center. A customer called and I answered the call expecting to take his order. I placed his order for him and afterwards, he said to me, ma'am, read *Isaiah 45:1-3* when you get a chance, but I want to tell you, just as God anointed and called King Cyrus by name, God is calling you. I decree a Cyrus anointing upon you in Jesus' Name. I was a little stunned, but graciously said Amen. Stunned because this has never happened to me before. I wasn't new to the Faith in Jesus Christ, as I was learning a lot and getting understanding of my purpose. I just did understand the fullness of the scripture and what it means to me. Amen puts you in agreement with what God has spoken through His word or through a man or woman of God. When I got home and read it, I still didn't have a full understanding of revelation until now. Everything is beautiful in its time, God's time. As you continue to study this passage of scripture and get it into your heart, remember the 7 promises of God in the scripture concerning you:

1. God would hold his right hand to subdue nations and loose the armor of Kings
2. To open before him the double doors which shall remain open
3. For his sake the Lord would make crooked places straight
4. To break the gates of brass because of him
5. Because of him, the Lord would cut asunder the bars of iron
6. To give him the treasures of darkness
7. To give him the hidden riches of secret places

Prayer:

Lord, open the eyes of the one reading this now, open their eyes to see things they cannot normally see, so they can claim things that would otherwise be unclaimed. I pray for them in the name of Jesus Christ, that this anointing and favor that located King Cyrus would fall on them too, to walk through the perfect will of God for their lives. I call forth the Cyrus anointing to be upon them even now, I activate it in the realm of the spirit. I thank you that they receive it by faith. Father, I thank you that you have predestined them before the foundation of the earth to reveal hidden treasures of darkness and riches to be found in secret places. Father, I pray that boldness is their portion, fear has no room because you have given them power, love, and a sound mind. I activate the battle axe grace upon their lives as you have made them a sharp weapon of warfare willing to be used by you to break the nations into pieces. Father, I thank you for raising up liberators, that will set the captives free, you have raised them up to be builders, I release the anointing to be master builders in Jesus's name. Thank you, Father, for restoring what had been stolen, I thank you Father for anointing those to receive wealth and resources to fulfill prophecy, in Jesus' name.

Time of Reflection:

Decree

As one that carries wealth, you must understand that your words have power. Yes, death and life is in the power of the tongue (Proverbs 18:21). Whatever your heart/mind is housing, you will speak (Luke 6:45 and Matthew 12:34). If your heart is full of bitterness, resentment, and anger, you will speak negatively of everything you encounter. In other words, you may be in transition, on your way to your wealthy place and where you are at this very moment seems like a drought. I promise you, if you continue in the faith, decreeing and confessing God's word, you will see changes. God will begin to present opportunities to you. This is where you do not talk yourself out of it. It is called self-sabotage. We can easily do that by not believing the opportunity is not for us and will shy away by not showing any interest or showing up. I guarantee you, that God has given you a creative idea and you push back because of fear. There you didn't show up for the meeting/the discovery call/zoom meeting, whatever the case is, the opportunity was lost. Know that opportunities are coming back around. Some of you have grieved over missed opportunities, God is saying grieve no more. There's a window opening where these opportunities will come around again. Restoration is here which comes with the ability to discern the opportunity and restoration comes with wisdom and the precision needed to move upon what was missed beforehand, just be ready. Decree over your life, your family, children, marriage, finances, business, and ministry. You have the authority to do so.

Declare this with me:

I decree and declare, I am wealthy! I am debt free! I live in the supernatural and in favor of God. Everything I put my hands to prospers, because I have been made unto good works in Jesus' name.

Did you know that when you decree a thing, it shall be established to you? Anything according to the word of God that you decree will be established. Let me put it like this, whatever you desire, the bible says, that God will give you the desires of your heart. The principle to that is you must delight yourself in Him, meaning what you desire cannot be for selfish motive and God wants you to be happy and excited about delighting yourself in Him.

The bible also declares that a light shall shine upon thy ways. We need the light of God's word to lead and guide us, the word tells us his word is spirit and it is life.

I do not know anyone that will take a road trip without putting the destination location in their GPS. I cannot take a road trip to a place I have never been before and do not use the GPS. I would be lost.

Job 22:28 KJV Thou shalt also decree a thing, and it shall be established unto thee, and the light shall shine upon thy ways.

Job 22:28 NKJV You will also declare a thing, and it will be established for you, so light will shine on your ways,

Job 22:28 NIV What you decide on will be done, and light will shine on your ways.

Job 22:28 AMP You will also decide and decree a thing, and it will be established for you, and the light of Gods favor will shine upon your ways.

My goodness, do you hear this, the scripture says, when you decide and decree.

Decides means to determine or settle, persuaded, or convince or conclude.

Decree in the bible dictionary means laws, an official command, or edict issued by a king or other person of authority. The decrees of the kings were often delivered to distant towns or cities by messengers and officially announced at city gates or public places.

The bible also refers to Gods decrees, universal laws, or rules to which the entire world is subject.

There's so much power in Gods' word and within us through the power of the Holy Ghost. Often, we are so distracted with life's problems and issues of the heart. The enemy will stop at nothing to get you distracted and focused on the wrong thing. Hear me, you must make up your mind and you must decide that enough is enough. Be done with living small, living with limitations and barriers. The bible tells us that we will have tribulation, but to be of good cheer because Jesus our Lord has overcome the world. He has given us an overcoming grace and anointing to conquer every attack of the enemy. Do not ever forget that greater is he that is in you, that he that is in the world.

I remember a time when I would believe God for healing and deliverance for individuals near and dear to my heart. I would pray and intercede, anoint them with anointing oil when they came in my presence. At the same time, the enemy was bombarding my mind with images of death. This can become daunting and tormenting, if you let it. I say this to you because if it is happening to me, I know that it is happening to you. Just do not succumb to the demonic suggestion of the enemy, if you do, you are literally agreeing with him. Agree with God and partner with the Holy Spirit concerning the words of healing, restoration, redemption, salvation and much more.

Make your decrees and declarations:

Time of Reflection

CHAPTER 4

WISDOM OF GOD FOR WEALTH

James 1:5 NIV

If any of you lacks wisdom, you should ask God, who gives generously to all without finding fault, and it will be given to you.

The word wisdom in the Greek is Sof-ee'ah, and that means, a broad and full of intelligence, used of the knowledge of remarkably diverse matters, being skilled in the management of affairs.

By wisdom James is talking not only about knowledge but about the ability to make wise decisions, even in difficult circumstances. Whenever we need wisdom, we can pray to God, and he will generously supply what we need. We do not have to grope in darkness, hoping to stumble upon answers. We can ask for Gods' wisdom to guide our choices.

Wisdom also means practical discernment. It begins with respect for God and increased ability to tell right from wrong. God is willing to give us this wisdom, but we will be unable to receive it if our goals are self-centered instead of God centered.

In this hour we need the wisdom of God. We can no longer operate in matters without sound wisdom. We can ask God and He will give it to us.

So why is wisdom important for the intercessor and what does that have to do with wealth?

Always know that first and foremost that wisdom is the principal thing, the scriptures tell us this in *Proverbs 4:7*

Wisdom is the principal thing, therefore get wisdom, and with all thy getting get understanding.

The Hebrew word for principal is ray-sheeth' part of the speech is noun, this means the beginning, first, chief or choice part. It also means order or rank.

You notice in the book of proverbs, there are over 50 scriptures dealing with wisdom and wisdom is referred to as "she". How is this significant? It is not, but I wanted the reader to be informed.

Let me give you two scripture denoting wisdom as "she"

Proverbs 1:20

Wisdom crieth without, she uttereth her voice in the streets.

Proverbs 2:1-5

My son, if you will receive my words and treasure my commandments within you, v2 so that your ear is attentive to skillful and godly wisdom and apply your heart to understanding seeking it conscientiously and striving for it eagerly, v 3 Yes, if you cry out for insight, and lift up your voice for understanding, v4, if you seek skillful and godly wisdom as you would silver and search for her as you would hidden treasures, v5 then you will understand reverent fear of the Lord, that is worshiping Him and regarding Him as truly awesome and discover the knowledge of God

Proverbs 9:1

Wisdom hath builded her house, she hath hewn out her seven pillars.

So here we see that wisdom is associated with building and she has a voice/influence. We are to seek godly wisdom, the wisdom of God that is from above, not worldly wisdom. Seeking Godly wisdom shows our dependence on God alone.

Wisdom is needed as you are unlocking wealth and prosperity within you. Your gifts and talents are being unlocked as you move fearlessly in the ordained wealthy place God has for you. Wisdom will be needed in this hour. Why is this so important? Because wisdom and humility keep you from pride and keeps you grounded in Him. As you are building and gaining wealth, it is easy to get caught up with the influences of the world.

Proverbs 9:1 speaks of building and seven pillars, which are:

1. Fear of the Lord
2. Instruction
3. Knowledge
4. Understanding
5. Discretion
6. Counsel
7. Reproof

These pillars speak of the very foundation of wisdom. Therefore, we need Godly wisdom in this hour especially to those that are called in the marketplace because you will meet many that do not know your God. Entrepreneurs will have business partners or associates that do not know the love or healing power of God. But through you, others will see the light of God that resides with you. The seven pillars must be your foundation as they carry substance and authenticity at its core. The wealth of an intercessor will be able to thrive off these pillars and its principles. Substance is needed in this season of your life for the purposes and will of God to be carried out if you are to walk in your wealthy place. When you have substance, you have sustainability and the ability to multiply. Intercessors entail substance, this includes the posture of your heart, humility, grace, wisdom, and courage. Let's look at each pillar.

The Fear of the Lord is a reverential awe which leads the believer to love and obey God. When the bible says that the fear of the Lord is the beginning of knowledge Proverbs 1:7, it means that a healthy respect for the living God is the foundation of religious faith and morality. The nature and outcome of a reverential awe of God is most clearly expressed in the words of *Deut 10:12-13*. God admonishes Israel to fear Him, describing that fear in terms of the lifestyle and attitudes it creates, scriptures says "And now, Israel, what does the Lord your God ask of you, but to fear the Lord your God, to walk in all His ways, to love Him, to serve the Lord your God with all your heart and with all your soul, and to observe the Lord's commands and decrees that I am giving you today for your own good"

The New Testament also views a reverent awe of God as a motive for holy living in *1 Peter 2:17*, honor all men, love the brotherhood. Fear God. Honor the King. Jesus taught that fear of God frees us from other fears. Jesus contrasts the anxiety of the pagan who worries about food and clothing, with freedom experienced by the believer who knows Gods' fatherly love. Fear of God offers us freedom from work and release from other concerns that block us from seeking first Gods' Kingdom and righteousness *Matthew 6:33*. The person who fears the Lord and has an awareness of Gods' power and authority will live a godly life out of respect for God.

Instruction is to furnish with information and with orders or directions. *Proverbs 19:20* says, "hear counsel, and receive instructions, that thou mayest be wise in thy latter end". Many do not like to submit to instructions or directions, however *Proverbs 4:13* tells us ``Take fast hold of instruction, let her not go, keep her, for she is thy life". Pride keeps people from listening and following instructions, especially in the affairs of their own life. They want to do life on their own terms without no one butting in. There is a downfall to those that do not like to heed to instructions, *Proverbs 5:23*, "He shall die without instructions, and in the greatness of his folly he shall go astray". It is so imperative that intercessors humble themselves, if you are to carry the riches of Gods' Glory and walk in your wealthy place, heed to instructions concerning your life, business deals, investments, and all aspects of your life. You are forever learning and growing.

Knowledge is the possession of facts, *Proverbs 2:5-6* tells us "that then shalt thou understand the fear of the Lord and find the knowledge of God, for the Lord giveth wisdom, out of his mouth cometh knowledge and understanding". Intercessors thrive on knowledge, as they need it to effectively execute Gods' assignment.

Understanding is the interpretation of facts, to perceive the meaning of, grasp the idea of and comprehend. *Psalm 119* is full of scriptures concerning understanding, *Proverbs 4:7b*, says" and with all your acquiring, get understanding actively seek spiritual discernment, mature comprehension, and logical interpretation" I truly believe these are days where we must press into God. When we yield to actively seek Gods' heart, mind and will on a matter, He will show His people the path of righteousness. Trusting God is a strong component of understanding. *Proverbs 3:5* tells us to "trust in and rely confidently on the Lord with all of our heart and do not rely on your own insight or understanding".

Discretion means the power or right to decide or act according to one's own judgment, it also means the quality of being discreet, prudence or decorum. Discretion is almost a lost art among us. However, we must get back to the purity of the heart. *Psalm 112:5*, Good will come to those who are generous and lend freely, who conduct their affairs with justice (discretion). Intercessors can discern when discretion is needed in certain matters. The enemy would love nothing more than to make a mockery of Gods' people. Let discretion and prudence rein in your hearts as you move into deeper realms in God. Having wealth requires discretion. You cannot be unwise and wealthy.

Counsel is advising or directing. In the Old Testament counsel given by advisers typically takes the form of a plan to deal with a specific situation. *Proverbs 15:22* says plans fail for lack of counsel, but many with advisers they succeed. We must understand that God's direction is rooted in his purposes. What God says to us reveals what he intends to do. Following Gods' counsel leads us into His good purpose. *Psalm 32:8* says I will instruct you and teach you in the way you should go, I will counsel you and watch over you. Gods' counsel never fails and never leads anyone astray. Counsel is a great substance an intercessor can hold, why? Because intercessors stand before the Lord to receive counsel or direction. *Psalm 16:7*, says I will bless the Lord, who hath given me counsel, my reins also instruct me in the night seasons. It is a blessing to receive the counsel of the Lord as He leads and directs you to your wealthy place. In the New Testament, Jesus introduced the Holy Spirit as the Counselor, the Greek word translated counselor is parakletos, who comes alongside to comfort, encourage, invite, or exhort. God said we are never left without guidance or help.

Reproof is the act of rebuking and even though many do not like it because it buffets the flesh, it is needed for growth, maturity, and wisdom. *Proverbs 15:10* says correction is grievous unto him that forsaketh the way, and he that hateth reproof shall die. The lack of receiving reproof only stagnant the intercessor. *Proverbs 6:23* says for the commandment is a lamp and the law is light, and the reproof of instructions are the way of life. Intercessor you will live after the reproof.

I know I spoke a lot about the wealthy place. We find it in scripture in *Psalm 66:12* amp, says you made men (charioteers) ride over our heads (in defeat) we went through the fire and through water, yet you brought us out into a broad place of abundance (wealthy place) to be refreshed.

The wealth of an intercessor is called to the wealthy place, to occupy this place, and to be refreshed. You will not fail as you embrace the seven pillars, wealth, and prosperity. Many of you have gone through much in life. Disappointments, divorce, loss of loved ones, heartache, hurt, and pain that almost suck the life out of you. Whatever pain you went through in life almost killed the vision and dreams you had. Your testimony is a testament to Gods' goodness and faithfulness. *Romans 8:28* declares that we know that all things work together for good to them that love God, to them who are the called according to his purpose. My prayer for you is that you are whole, that you have soundness of mind and joy unspeakable joy as you walk in your wealthy place. Myles Munroe once said when you believe in your dream and your vision, then it begins to attract its own resources, no one is born to be a failure. He also penned this statement, "The wealthiest place in the world is not the gold mines of South America or the oil fields of Iraq or Iran. They are not diamond mines in South Africa or the banks of the world. The wealthiest place on the planet is just down the road. It is the cemetery. There lie buried companies that were never started, inventions that were never made, bestselling books that were never written, and masterpieces that were never planted. In the cemetery are buried the greatest treasures of untapped potential. Ponder on this for a moment and reflect on what you may have not tapped into concerning your gifts and talents. I remember God showed me in a dream the words written in big bold letters "TREASURES WITHIN" I often ponder on those words because it gives me hope and I keep moving forward even in the face of uncertainty and ostacles. Beloved, you are a treasure and you have treasures within you that are waiting to be released that will beautify your sphere of influence.

Prayer:

Father, I thank you for your intercessors, even as they carry substance of these seven pillars, I pray they are catapulted to their wealthy place. I break all ties of the old and destroy every demonic cycle that has held them in bondage. I decree they are the curse breaker in their bloodline. I pray that as they embrace these pillars, I decree it is a strong foundation for them and they will never to be removed from their post and calling. Father I pray, that holy spirit will begin to bring to their remembrance of dreams and visions they once had, that they begin to take it off the shelf. I pray that you breathe life into what they once believed. Awaken them to their potential, awaken them to new dimensions Father. Even now God, I break and destroy depression, sabotage, and every false vision that the enemy is trying to infiltrate into their spirits, I decree your intercessors are not failures, and I unbox them even now, leaders that tried to stick them only in one place, I break and destroy limitations and barriers that was set against them and declare freedom in Jesus' name, amen.

Time of Reflection

CHAPTER 5

HELP, I DON'T FEEL QUALIFIED.

You are qualified! Why? Because you are a believer of Jesus Christ. You will deal with people that will say, you cannot speak on something you have no authority. I believe that is true to a certain extent, but what if it was God inspired? What if from the beginning of time, God placed the seed of wealth inside of you, he placed a message inside of you to teach and preach? What if you carry the word of deliverance in your belly? Yes, this comes with discipline and maturation. I have seen people not walk in their call because they did not feel qualified by way of their own misplaced emotions/thought patterns or someone speaking negatively over their lives. In any case, God is a redeemer, and He will redeem the time. I also believe that God will place you in a different atmosphere to expose you to something new. You will have a taste of it, enough to open your eyes to wanting to learn more. When we look deeper into why people would say, they are not qualified or worthy of wealth and prosperity. We find that some deal with a scarcity mindset. This type of mindset is obsessed with a lack or something, usually money, possessions, or time. The mind is everything, what you think you become. Mindset is a critical component of success in every area of life, whether it is in business, ministry, or marriage. There is research that reveals that those with more positive beliefs around aging live 7.5 years longer than those with less positive self-perceptions of aging. So basically, your mindset can prolong your life. In other words, your mindset sets the tone for success in your life. Scarcity mentality refers to people seeing life as a finite pie, so that if one person takes a big piece, that leaves less for everyone else. What are you thinking and speaking? Are you consistently speaking positive or negative words over your life or situation? *Proverbs 6:2* Thou are snared with the words of thy mouth, thou are taken with the words of thy mouth. Snared means to lure, entice, caught by a bait, to be entrapped, or to be taken by a noose. The words that you speak frame your world, whether they are positive or negative. It is time to make positive confessions over your life regardless of what you are facing right now. Confession in the Greek is homologeo which means to say the same thing as another, to agree with, to declare, to praise and celebrate. You must say the same thing God is saying (in His Word). Confessing who you are in Christ Jesus. This way the mind and heart is agreeing with the word of God. When it is done on a consistent basis, you'll begin to see changes in your behavior and speech. Do not get me wrong, the enemy will still try to bully you, however you must remain steadfast in confessing and declaring the word of God. You are not your situation, you are not the bad decision, you are not your past. Do not allow the enemy to come after your voice to shut you down. Your voice is powerful, and it carries weight in the realm of the spirit. When you go through a season of warfare, this is the best place to release words of life, why? Because words are a creative force, you are creative and innovating, so of course the enemy will try to stop you, but he cannot, because he does not want you to give birth, to bring forth the destiny of God for your lives, even that of your bloodline. Remember you are the curse breaker. Even now I sense the Lord is causing the voice of His people to return to them. I am telling you; you are a force to be reckoned with. I see the confidence of the Lord rising in you again. The blockage has been removed and you are no longer stuck. Release the praises of God out of your mouth, breakthrough is in your mouth, wealth is in your mouth, prosperity is in your mouth, healing is in your mouth. So do not allow the adversity and situation in your life steal your voice again, lift your voice like a triumph and shout unto God and watch the trajectory of your life change as you let the ruach breath of God flow in and through you. I also sense that voices were taken at a very young age. The attack came by way of abuse, sexual, physical, and verbal abuse and it has not only taken away your voice, but your identity and many are living their lives not fulfilled, even believers of Jesus Christ. As one that has been molested as a child, I had to learn a lot about myself when I was an adult and saw the impact of the abuse. When it is not dealt with, arrested development sneaks in, rejection and abandonment come in. we build walls to protect ourselves from ever getting hurt again, we tend not to have successful relationships with the opposite sex. We can be too clingy or not affectionate enough. Therefore, we can think things like am I qualified? Am I enough, or am I good enough? Abuse can warp the self-perception of the person. But God, his wisdom and healing power is no match for what the enemy has tried to drown people in. These are the days and even now that restoration has hit you and your household, physically, mentally, spiritually, and financially. Not only restoration beloved intercessor, but recompense and retribution for all your suffering. No longer suffer in silence. Receive the healing gift of the Holy Ghost to heal your soul. You can now breathe easy, go forth and uncover the treasures of darkness and hidden riches in secret places. It is time to walk in your wealthy place.

Prayer:

Father, I pray in the name of Jesus' that you arise over your intercessors with healing in your wings, heal every area of their lives! I declare that restoration has come onto them, no longer returning to the place of bondage. I thank you Lord for restoring their voice, their confidence, their hope and faith in you and what they have been called to do, I pray that they will begin to speak the words that edify and encourage themselves, even as David had to encourage himself. Father, I break and destroy every blockage and time-release attack of the enemy concerning your intercessors. I cover them in the blood of Jesus Christ and release a wall of fire all around about them and their household in the name of Jesus. Be magnified in the earth O God, as your intercessors release praise and adoration unto you. As in the days of Jehoshaphat, I pray that your intercessors will begin to sing and to praise you that will cause an ambushment against their enemies, Father, I pray, that you arise and cause your enemies to be scattered in the name of Jesus, and I declare that the souls of your intercessors are delivered, healed and whole in the name of Jesus, amen.

Time of Reflection

CHAPTER 6

REFINED FOR WEALTH

Refine means to bring to a fine or pure state, free from impurities, to purify from what is coarse, vulgar or debasing.

We all must go through purification, our whole journey is about being purified, cleansed in our hearts. The whole gest of manifesting wealth and prosperity is because you must give God permission to tell you what to do with your wealth. It is all about the Kingdom of God and your assignment in the earth to advance His Kingdom. It is about glorifying and worshipping God with what he has bestowed upon you.

The reason some can get thousands upon thousands of monies and blow it in a short period of time is because, they didn't give it an assignment, their minds were still poverty stricken, no knowledge of investments into property, not giving to the poor etc. God has created a wealth generating system that cannot fail. We know that money answers all things *(Ecc 10:19)*. The first reaction to that statement by many Christians would be that it is carnal, selfish, and outside of biblical values, yet is a direct quote from the bible in *Ecc 10:19*. Money is an essential thing in this life, so the desire for money is not selfish, it is necessary. The church building cannot pay for itself, doing a conference cannot pay for itself, nor is walking the streets to evangelize, which does not take much money, but you still need provision for food, clothing, and shelter, you still need money. There are a couple of reasons that I can mention as to why God wants you to have money and the right mindset for money. One, to fund kingdom work, the word of God tells us to go into all the world and preach the gospel (*Matthew 24:14* and *Mark 16:15*) and two, to subdue the earth, to have dominion on the earth *(Genesis 1:28)*, we should be controlling the resources. In this same passage of scripture of *Genesis 1:28*, God said to bless them, be fruitful and multiply, this doesn't sound like God does not want his people to be in lack or poverty. However, we must align our thinking about wealth with Gods so we can operate within His system. If you're ready for a change in your financial situation, begin to study the scriptures concerning wealth and prosperity. I want to open your eyes to let you know you are called to wealth. This book is not a how to get rich, it is a book to help you identify root causes of lack and poverty, it is to help you change your mindset that wealth is for you, it is for you to go deeper into your study and prayer time concerning the seed of wealth within you that will change the course of your life and that of your household, and for you to know what to do with wealth as it relates to advancing Gods' Kingdom in the earth, and lastly to unlock the endless flow of possibilities through your gifts and talents in occupying whatever seven mountains you have been called to. Let me make mention here what those seven mountains are:

1. Religious Mountain
2. Family Mountain
3. Education Mountain
4. Governmental Mountain
5. Media Mountain
6. Arts and Entertainment Mountain
7. Business Mountain

At least five of the seven cultural mountains can be categorized as the workplace. The mountains of government, business, education, arts and entertainment and media all fit the billing of career oriented, professional environments. The remaining two Religious and Family Mountain though not purely work surroundings, but have a definite vocations aspect to them, moms and full-time senior leaders are working, not in a corporate setting, but what they do is work. Entrepreneurs and those in Network Marketing are part of the Business Mountain, so they spend the majority of their time in the workplace as well, even if it is a home office.

Getting back to Gods' system of wealth, I said it is the fund the kingdom work, to subdue the earth and it is also to provide well for you and your household. As God is refining you and your mindset for this shift, you must rid all other ideologies of the purpose of money, wealth, and prosperity. God is calling you to be the solution and to have the answer for those that are in need. You must align your heart to the heartbeat of the Father, which means when He tells you to give and the amount to give, there will be no hesitation. When He tells you what to invest in, what property to buy or build, you will do it out of obedience. God wants you to see wealth from His perspective. You must know that God is your sole source, *Phil 4:19* tells us, and my God shall supply all your needs according to His riches in Glory by Christ Jesus. The idea is simple, yet it takes a lot of spiritual work to get to the place where you let God be your sole source of supply. The bible tells us, if someone won't work, he should not eat (*2 Thessalonians 3:10*) and God is creator of work, he never intended for us to put our faith and hope in our labor alone and he never intended for you to turn anything else into your source, not your credit cards, the government, and so on. He is your source of supply. God supplies everything you need to thrive, He supplies the power to produce wealth, and He supplies the blessing that produces wealth. The Blessing is the empowerment to prosper. God has bestowed His Blessing on you beloved. When you think about it, the bible does not say God makes you wealthy, it says He will give you the power the produce wealth *(Duet 8:18)* that means, He will always give you something to put your hands to anoint your ability and bring the BLESSING on display when you are obedient to His commands. I remember reading an article from Buddy Pilgrim, he said the key to allowing God to be your source is to first know your calling, then to stay focused on your calling and finally execute your calling with a faithful heart. I must admit, procrastination has gotten me into trouble many times. Many people deal with procrastination and must forge ahead without hesitation.

I believe wholeheartedly that when we study scriptures concerning our mandate in the earth, we will have a fresh outlook from Gods' point of view. The last thing I want to point out in this, as God is refining you, know that (Kingdom) business is the only system that creates wealth, not working 2 or 3 jobs. *Luke 19:13 ESV* says, engage in business until I come. We tend to want the wealth transfer spoken of in *Proverbs 13:22* to be an event. But Gods' system is an ongoing system, a continual flow of wealth into the hands of the righteous. Business is that system. That does not mean every person is called to own a business but each one will engage in business in one form or another, whether at our jobs, or with investments. You may be called to own or manage a business in some way. As Christians, we are called to take dominion and business is a powerful place of influence in this world that should be dominated by the righteous. Another way we participate in God's system of business is by acting as patrons. When you give your money to a business, you are transferring wealth from the Kingdom of light to whatever that business stands for and if you own a business, you are bringing money from the sinner into the realm of righteousness. The way in which we treat another man's business (his system of wealth creation) will determine the success you see in your own wealth. *Luke 16:12* says if you have not been faithful in what is another man, who will give you what is your own, something to heed to.

Prayer:

Father, I pray that your intercessor will submit to the refining as you are preparing your people for the wealth transfer. I pray that your people will understand what this really means. Father, I break and destroy by the fire of God, the spirits of slothfulness and procrastination. I release unto your intercessors an urgency to move forward. I break the lazy spirit that causes them to put off doing work for another day. Father I pray, a renewal of strength, vitality, and the spirit of might to come upon your people. Release unto them, witty invention, and creative ideas. I pray that the business plans are written and clearly articulate the heart of serving others in the name of Jesus. I pray those that you called to rule and dominate in one or several of the seven mountains, that you give them insight and influence in the name of Jesus. I pray that your people will have a healthy perspective of money and doing business righteously in the name of Jesus, I pray that integrity rules and stewardship will be their portion in the name of Jesus, I release the wisdom of God upon every entrepreneur that is building, every manager that is managing in the name of Jesus, amen.

Time of Reflection:

CHAPTER 7

ABRAHAM- A MAN OF OBEDIENCE AND WEALTH

When we meet Abraham in scripture, he is following the voice of God to a city whose founder and builder was God.

At this point, Abraham had not heard of this city, and it required him to leave his kindred behind (*Genesis 12:1-3*). We see the promise that God made to Abram, God told him, I will make of thee a great nation, I will bless thee and make thy name great, and thou shall be a blessing, he also promised Abram in v3, I will bless them that bless thee, and curse him that curseth thee, and in all the families of the earth shall be blessed. We can trust God's provision when He gives us instructions. Many times, we look for confirmation and nothing is wrong with that, but when you look for ten confirmations and still not moving forward or seeking God, there is a problem. However, when we move on what God says, it yields a great return from the Lord.

This one decision would allow him to not only access the promise and promotion, but it would be the unveiling of him as a prophet and intercessor (*Genesis 20:7*)

What this helps to unveil is the idea that there is a promise tied to intercession, but this promise is not predicated on how well we are able to articulate the scriptures to unlock it. It is not founded on the idea that there is a particular formula the intercessor must pray to access the wealthy place, but rather we understand that the intercessor through a life of obedience accesses the promised place where God dwells, and Gods promise of wealth and provision. The scripture reminds us that there is a place in God that "eye hath not seen, ear hath not heard." These are times where God is unveiling this to us. We are in times where there is an earnest expectation of the creature is in waiting for the manifestation of the sons of God. We must have a posture of obedience at all costs. Our obedience is not just about us, but our lineage, our posterity.

Abrahams' one act of obedience put him in position to later sit and talk with God as friends and intercede for a city God would soon judge. It would be this friendship with God that would make even God say "how can I do this without revealing it to my friend Abraham? (*Genesis 18:17-21*).

Abrahams' consistent obedience, even during the toughest times of his life, unlocked for him the promise. These promises were not just simply for him, but these promises would impact generations. These promises would provide the framework for various religions and give us the blueprint by which we operate not only by faith, but true obedience as an intercessor.

Abraham's visitation with God, and willingness to give not only of himself but of his possessions unlock for him the wealthy place. God was able to commune with Abraham. His willingness to invite God into his life to take up residency, allowed God to search his heart and know him. In knowing Abraham, as one would a friend, he couldn't help but to respond to Abrahams' desperate desires to please

Him, even when Abraham made mistakes. It was through this type of intimacy in which God showed him the stars and promised his children would outnumber them.

There is a beautiful place found in intercession that goes beyond warfare and toil. There is a place in intercession where the intercessor learns to hear God's voice and God hears the voice of the intercessor. It is in this knowing of each other that true legislative authority is birthed. It is also in this place of transaction and transformation that God, the glorious Father, and friend that he is, pulls back the curtain that separates the intercessor from provision and unlocks wealth.

When God pulled back this curtain for Abraham, God spoke these things concerning him.

1. You are a great and mighty nation.
2. All the nations will bless you.
3. I know you.
4. You will command your children.
5. You will command your household.

It should be the goal of the intercessor to hear these words spoken concerning their life. It is through these words/promises of God in which we begin to access the wealthy place of God. God continues to be faithful to us even now as we are the seed of Abraham. We see Abraham's character and relationship with God. We have a wonderful example of their relationship. Obedience is key in this hour, the bible tells us in Isaiah 1:19, if ye be willing and obedient, ye shall eat the good of the land. What is it that you must leave behind and follow God? We can glean a lot from the history of Abraham. He plays an important role in the Christian faith. It was Abraham whom God chose to be the father of many nations, simply because it was His will. I hope that you are encouraged to see the benefits of a relationship with Abba Father. When I speak of benefits, it is not just what you can get out of it, but it is the blossoming and nurturing aspect of a relationship. God loves to be loved on and He loves to love on you.

I believe one of the things we tend to think is that we will be doing what God called us to do in our strength and ability, even as it relates to walking in obedience, yes it takes a made-up mind to say yes to God and literally say, I am going to obey God. God can work with that. *Philippians 2:13* amp clearly tells us, for it is (not your strength but it is) God who is effectively at work in you, both to will and to work (that is, strengthening, energizing, and creating in you the longing and the ability to fulfill your purpose) for His good pleasure. Beloved intercessor, you are not alone, and you do not have to do what God has called you to do in your own strength. God is working in you; all you need to do is yield and submit to walking this out in obedience and faith. Abraham trusted God, he believed God. Be reminded, that you are a spirit filled believer, and *Phil 1:6* declares being confident of this very thing, that he which hath begun a good work in you will perform it until the day of Jesus Christ and what God is about to do in you and through you will not be by might, nor by power, but by his spirit concerning you. You must understand that God formed a covenant with Abraham, of all men on earth, the Lord chose this faithful man to become the father of a covenant people. A covenant is an agreement in which two parties make commitments to each other. Each party takes upon himself, as part of his acceptance of the covenant, certain obligations that pertain to the relationship. We enter into sacred agreements with God, promising our obedience to his will, in turn, he has promised glorious blessings to us if we obey and serve him.

I prophesy, that you are in the days where God is girded up with strength, mentally and emotionally to break away from places of familiarity. Even as Abram left his father's house, I see a day has come upon you to get up and move, for some geographically, for some your mindset has shifted, you are no longer satisfied on the level that you have been in. These are the days where God is saying ascend and come up higher. This means leaving family and friends on the level they refuse to leave. Make the necessary adjustments, said God as you have been commissioned to transition. You will feel a refreshing come upon you even as you obey God. Your prayer life is reviving, your dreams are reviving, what you thought you lost and being returned to you said God. You will once again occupy and be engaged with me, said God. No more distractions, your focus has returned back to you, your belly is stirring even now, I prophesy that rivers of living water are stirring even now, I see the dam breaking forth. A strong release of creativity, insight, illumination, fresh oil, new wine and new wine skin has come upon you said God.

Also, the Lord says He has given you strength to let it all go, the bitterness, anger and disappointment and the grace to walk in love and thankfulness. What you are about to walk into is without toil, it is being released unto you now. New, New, New said God, the new awaits you, it is being released to you with ease, nothing forced in this season and hour and there will be a natural cohesiveness and diving connections said the Lord. Now give God a shout of praise as you receive this word.

Prayer

Father, I Pray in the name of Jesus, I believe God's word, I am what the word says I am. I am the righteousness of God, a new creation and heir of God and a joint heir with Jesus, I have been redeemed by the blood of the lamb and redeemed from the curse of the law, redeemed from sickness, disease, poverty, and death. I declare I can do all things through Christ who strengthens me, I am more than a conqueror. I declare the faith of God dwells in me and through it I have the victory that overcomes the world. I thank you Father that I have an obedient spirit and it is you who is working in me both to will and do of your good pleasure. I decree, Lord, that as you have called me out from among them, that the blessing of the Lord is upon me and no sorrow is added in Jesus' name, amen.

Time of Reflection

CHAPTER 8

FAITH FOR WEALTH

Hebrews 11:1 KJV

Now faith is the substance of things hoped for, the evidence of things not seen.

Hebrews 11:1 TLB

What is faith? It is the confident assurance that something we want is going to happen. It is the certainty that what we hope for is waiting for us, even though we cannot see it up ahead.

Hebrews 11:1 NIV

Now faith is the confidence in what we hope for and assurance about what we do not see.

Assurance means a positive declaration intended to give confidence, freedom from doubt and believe in one's ability.

Hope means the feeling that what is wanted can be had or that events will turn out for the best.

The Greek word for hope is el-pid'-zo, G1679 and it means to wait for salvation (deliverance) with joy and full confidence.

God has already written your destiny. He has already made you wealthy. You just need to pull it down by faith! Wow what a powerful statement. You must know that it is more than a statement, it is truth.

First let us define faith. What is faith? Faith is the ability to believe God, both trust His character and to take His word as true and reliable. Faith is belief, confidence, trust, and reliance.

In the word of God, religious faith is a life shaping attitude toward God. The person with faith considers God's revelation of himself to be truth and sure. So, the person with faith, responds to God with trust, love, and obedience.

Intercessors must have total trust and dependence on God and the Word of God.

Mark 11:24 tells us whatever you ask for in prayer, believe that you have received it and it will be yours.

Many times, we pray and do not genuinely believe. We feel like if it happens, it happens and if it doesn't, oh well! That attitude and statement does not work in the Kingdom of God. We are speaking beings and must remember that life and death is in the power of the tongue *(Proverbs 18:21)* often times, we only stop at the first portion of that scriptures, but when you dig deeper into it, the word is literally saying you will eat the fruit of what you are saying:

Pro 18:21

Death and life are in the power of the tongue, and they that love it shall eat the fruit thereof.

The Amplified version says: Death and life are in the power of the tongue, and those who love it and indulge it will eat its fruit and bear the consequences of their words.

We can be so careless with words and at the end say things like, I was just playing! Or you may have spoken out of frustration concerning a matter. The good news is we can repent, plead the blood of Jesus, and speak righteously.

There is much to do within our souls as it relates to renewing the mind, healing, and deliverance. We must uproot old habits, mindsets, and thinking (small thinking).

God wants us to think BIG! Believe it or not, that is a struggle for many people.

Many of God's Intercessors are powerful prayer warriors but struggle greatly in the area of how they see themselves, the great things God has for them and how God wants to give them wealth and prosperity. Some are so bound by generational curses, poverty and by the spirit of religion. You will need to work your faith to manifest wealth and prosperity. The wealth of the Intercessors must thrive on their faith. Just as an intercessor work their faith in believing God for healing, deliverance, or breakthrough, you must work your faith concerning wealth and prosperity and whatever vehicle God uses to unlock it. God cares about your finances. Just as with anything else, you should approach your finances in faith, believing that your heavenly father will be true to his word. I was one that was believing God for finances, but it was from a religious standpoint. Meaning, I had no assignment for the money I was asking God for, other than to pay all my bills and to buy nice stuff, that's it. I just got tired of not having enough money and living from paycheck to paycheck. However, part of approaching your finances in faith involves the way you think and speak about them. If you constantly focus on your lack of money, complain about your financial outlook, and doubt that God will be faithful to his Word, then you will receive exactly what you expect. However, if you proclaim God's goodness, thank Him for His provision and expect Him to be faithful to his word, you will receive the provision from Him that you expect. Did you know faith and patience work together? *Hebrew 6:12* That ye be not slothful, but followers of them who through faith and patience inherit the promises *and James 1:4 AMP-* and let endurance (faith) have its perfect result and do a thorough work, so that you may be perfect and completely developed in your faith lacking nothing. We are commanded not the be slothful, in other words lazy. Some of us have strong mindset that does not allow us to follow a mentor or get advice from people that are in positions that we desire to go, that my friend is called pride. We can learn a lot from what others have gone through and how they persevered to another tax bracket status, being debt free, being a philanthropist, and much more including being happy and joyful in their lives.

Faith comes by hearing and hearing by the word of God, *Romans 10:17*, when we hear the word of God, the testimonials of others, it encourages us to keep going. Honestly at times, you will still need to push yourself to keep going, just remember the testimony, the promises of God, have a visual in front of you and keep believing, and speak words of encouragement to yourself. These are the formulas, believe it or not. It is quite simple, but we lose sight and get lazy and stop. Trust the supply of grace and strength to help you on your journey.

In order to inherit the promise, remember *Hebrew 6:12*, this is the intercessors' inheritance, it is through faith and patience. When we investigate the word inherit, in the Greek language it is the word keronomeo, keys 2816 and it means to receive a lot, to receive inheritance by right, or receive the portion assigned to you, or receive an allotted portion. As a child of God, you have received the inheritance. There are privileges that are given to a child of God/Intercessor; however, we must access them through faith, work the principles of God, prayer, worship, and obedience to God. I am sure that we all have experienced the pain of going ahead of God, that's why patience is so key. I truly believe you are on the timetable of God, so let patience have its perfect work with you. Confess who God is in your life, here are a few confessions that you can make:

1. God is more than enough; God will generously provide you all you need. Thank you will always have everything you need, and plenty left over to share with others, as the scriptures says, they share freely and give generously to the poor, their good deeds shall be remembered forever 2 *Corinthians 9:8-9*

2. Every need is covered; My God shall supply all your need according to his riches in glory in Christ Jesus *Philippians 4:19*

3. Overcoming debt; Owe nothing to anyone except for your obligation to love one another, if you love your neighbor, you will fulfill the requirements of Gods' law *Romans 13:8*

Right now, begin proclaiming the Lord's provision in your life. Let faith and patience work.

Prayer:

Father, I activate your intercessors in the realm of faith in the name of Jesus, I pray that faith and patience will have its perfect work in each of them, we know that faith is substance of things hope for the evidence of things not seen, I pray that you would open the eyes of your intercessors, that they are strengthen to walk by faith and not by sight. I pray that as they have faith for wealth and prosperity, that you would begin to do a work in their heart concerning patience. Let your intercessors not be weary in doing well, but I decree they shall reap a harvest if they faint not, in the name of Jesus. You said in your word Lord, Psalm 30: 6 as for me, in my prosperity, I said, I shall never be moved. Causes your intercessors to be steadfast, unmovable, always abounding in the work of the Lord. Cause them to be like trees firmly planted by the rivers of water in the name of Jesus. I pray for an activation of the wealth of the intercessor to emerge with boldness and every religious devil is bound in the name of Jesus, amen.

Beloved Intercessor of God, these are the days where the substance of God will be so rich and deep within you and the seed of wealth will blossom within you now and it will spring up said the Lord, This is a season that the glory and grace of God will rest upon you, and you will begin to have face to face encounters with me saith God, and from that place of encounters you will begin to be ignited by the fire of God for your place and assignment in the earth. You will have a clear direction, said the Lord, for I am dealing with the spirit of confusion and chaos as I move in your midst, said God to clear the path for you. Even as the spirit of the fear of the Lord rests upon you, you will fear no man said God, for perfect love cast out fear and I am love. I'm in your midst and fight on your behalf. No longer will you feel alone or abandoned, for I will bring you into a company of people that carry my heart and demonstrate the authenticity of my love and wisdom toward you, said the Lord. The Lord says, I will teach you how to trust again, for these are the days, where relationships will be paramount, no longer are you to function as a lone ranger. So, get ready, says God for the Wealth of the Intercessor to emerge on the scene and work the works of miracles, signs, and wonders. I release upon you the Supernatural's of God and you will know that it is not by might, nor power, but my spirit that I do a work in you and through said God. For these are the days where eyes have not seen, nor ears heard of what I am getting ready to do on the earth through you. No plague can stop the work that I have planned from the foundation of the earth. I call my people to arise and know that you are covered, said God and you will prosper, even during the pandemic.

Arise Prophetic Intercessors and let the Lion of the Tribe of Judah roar within you! Roar over poverty and lack, roar over fear, roar over limitations and barriers and break forth into your wealthy place in Jesus' name, amen.

TIME OF REFLECTION

Bonus

3 Majors Keys to Activating and Unlocking the Realm of Wealth Within the Intercessor

1 Chronicles 29:12-13 NIV

Wealth and honor come from you; you are the ruler of all things. In your hands are strength and power to exalt and give strength to all. Now our God, we give you thanks, and praise your glorious name.

Deuteronomy 8:18 NIV

But remember the Lord your God, for it is he who gives you the ability to produce wealth and so confirm his covenant, which he swore to your ancestors, as it is today.

We first must understand that wealth comes from God, and He wants you to be wealthy in every aspect of your life. You may be going through a tough time now, meaning, bills are stacking up, bank accounts are low or in the negative and you are wondering, how in the world, me God's Intercessor is living from paycheck to paycheck, not able to make ends meet. I have given my life over to prayer and intercessor, I have stood in the gap and prayed for others, heck I have seen my prayers manifest in their lives, and now they are living their best life. What happened? I pray for myself too; I have desires to see breakthroughs in my life as well.

You may be thinking, I have tried everything, from working 2 jobs, doing overtime, doing a side hustle, it seems like nothing is working for me. But you know within you, you have been called to be wealthy, you have been called to finance the advancement of God's Kingdom in the earth, you have been called to do the work of a Philanthropist. You may be thinking, I am creative, I have ideas, but what is this blockage, why do I feel stuck, why isn't the momentum there, where are the people and why do I feel like I have false starts? You may have had people that you look up to, but you realize, they do not genuinely believe in your vision as you believe in their vision. Wow, what a big disappointment. But you realize, at the end of the day, something must change and change for the better.

I want to share with you 3 principles to activating and unlocking the realm of wealth with you.

As Gods' intercessors, we tend to go hard for someone else and what tends to happen is they reap the spoils of your prayers, fasting and intercession. Nothing is wrong with that, but I have noticed, intercessors have been worn out and not really going to back for themselves as they do others. I guess it is that humility part of them. That is their nature, to be selfless.

I tell you; this is the season for the Intercessors to rise and shine! Your reward is at hand.

So let me share with you these three keys and as I share this, I want you to take it into prayer and intercession for yourselves. God is ready to perform His word concerning you.

Please know my fellow intercessor, that I have been praying for you. I always pray *Psalm 16:1* over your lives.

Psalm 16:1

Preserve me, O God, for in thee do I put my trust.

The Hebrew word for preserve is Shaw-mar H 8104, it means to keep, keeper, watchman, regard, save and watch. It also means to have charge of, guard, protect, save, retain, to celebrate.

Shaw-mar a primitive root, means properly hedge about, as with thorns, guard, generally protect.

Intercessors function from a Shamar grace, which means they protect, guard the house of God, so as does God, he protects and guards His Intercessors.

This is the season and hour where God is saying, I'm protecting you, guarding you, yes you have experienced many attacks, many disappointments, many set back, but my hand of protection has always been there, and this is the season where you will see the manifested promises that I promised you, for you and your children's children. God says you will see the manifested promises and you will live to enjoy them. You will leave a legacy for your children, says God, for I am a God of legacy.

Here are the 3 keys to activate and unlock the wealth within:

Wealth begins with a Mindset.

Key # 1.

Wealth is a choice (Because you must choose your mindset)

Philippians 2:5, Let this mind be in you, which was also in Christ Jesus.

So, when the bible tells us, LET this mind be in you, it is saying, for us to have understanding, to feel, to think as another individual, to be of one's party, side with Him. We are to side with Jesus Christ, as Christ had the mind of His Father. He always stated that he came to do the Will of His Father, which art in Heaven. He never deviated from that assignment.

Jesus Christ mindset is that of wealth, prosperity, health, blessing, wholeness, righteousness and much more that pertains to the Kingdom of God.

Romans 8:6, For to be carnally minded is death, but to be spiritually minded is life and peace.

Now we must understand that carnality in any aspect of our lives will end in death. Carnal mindset leads to poverty, lack, scarcity, dearth and not enough. It is an enemy to the blessing of God, to wealth, prosperity, and good health.

Intercessor, you must change your mindset. It does not matter your environment or the culture of which you grew up in. The Word of God trumps it all and has the capability to change your circumstance once you work the principles of the Word. Renewing your mind takes intentionality and boldness. You will go from small thinking to thinking BIGGER, beyond what you are accustomed to. You are in the Kingdom of God and there is no scarcity or lack in Gods' Kingdom. This will take time, but it is doable. Trust God.

Prayer:

Father, in Jesus' Name, I thank you for the intercessor that has made up their mind to change the way they think concerning wealth and prosperity for themselves. I praise you in advance that they are walking in the freedom and liberty of wealth. I activate and unlock the impossible that is within and stretch their capacity to think BIGGER, amen.

Key #2

Wealth is not something you run after; it is something you attract.

Alignment is taking place as you embrace that you are one that is called to advance Gods' Kingdom, you have been called to be a financier in the Kingdom of God. As you embrace this, know that you must also embrace the fact that God is raising you up to occupy the wealthy place. This means that as you obey God in every area of your life, including giving, you have been positioned to prosper and expand.

Luke 6:38, Give, and it shall be given unto you, good measure, pressed down and shaken together, and running over, shall men give into your bosom. For with the same measure that ye mete withal it shall be measure to you again.

Proverbs 3:9-10, Honor the Lord with thy substance, and the first fruits of all thine increase, so shall thy barns be filled with plenty, and thy presses shall burst out with new wine.

Giving attracts wealth to you. It is no doubt that God will not have his word return to Him void, but He is watching over it to perform it concerning you. Intercessors must have a heart of giving and be a generous giver

Prayer:

Father, I pray in the name of Jesus, that your intercessors have a heart to give. As they give, I prophesy, I continual flow of your anointing, flow of heaven's resources to come to them. I decree, that as they give, it will be given back to them, good measure, pressed down and shaken over. I pray that revelation will open to your intercessors concerning wealth as they give and let it activate and unlock the anointing to gain wealth. I pray that you will give them the blueprint for generational wealth in the name of Jesus. Amen.

Key # 3

You must Believe God and believe that Wealth is for you.

You attract wealth by believing what God says in His covenant. You are in covenant with God.

You must also develop a wealth perspective in both thoughts and words and act on it.

Please know that the key to wealth is not just money, but it is a mindset, it is thoughts and attitude. I briefly spoke about mindset earlier. What are your thoughts or belief system about wealth, what is your attitude towards it? Are you angry when you see people you know prospering, are you jealous when you see people living a lifestyle that you desire?

Sometimes we must check our hearts and attitude toward others that are in the space that we desire. I do not believe it is jealousy, but often we compare and say things like, goodness, they are not living for you God, how did they get ahead like that? This only means, we need to get before the Father and ask that he create in us a clean heart and renew a right spirit within us.

Proverbs 10:22, The Blessing of the Lord brings wealth without painful toil for it.

Wow, that scripture is loaded. It is your covenant right as a son/daughter of God to manifest the blessing of the Lord in your life. Years ago, I learned that the word blessing means, the power and means or the ability to prosper. It is God's favor and protection over your life. So, there is no reason to envy someone else because they are prospering, you are in covenant with God Almighty, you are the seed of Abraham. The Lord greatly blessed Abraham, he was rich, in flocks, herds, silver, gold, servants, camels and donkeys (*Genesis 24:35*).

The latter part of that scripture says without painful toil to it. I am telling you, when you believe, anything is possible. I also know that intercessors suffer much and now have concluded that they want all that God has for them. They have suffered much injustice, accusations, rejections, abandonment, self-sacrifice, being misunderstood, lied on, shame, reproach and much more.

God is removing the reproach, the witchcraft and control! Intercessors are now moving to the rhythm of Gods' heartbeat without fear and without reservation. There is a move of God that is releasing his intercessors into the realm of wealth, freedom, creativity, divine connections, and hearts are open to wisdom from other millionaires and entrepreneurs.

The substance and treasures within intercessors are unfolding even the more and it will make room for them to expand in every way possible to the glory of God and the advancement of the Kingdom of God.

2nd *Corinthians 9:8,* And God is able to make all grace (every favor and earthly blessing) come in abundance to you, so that you may always (under all circumstances, regardless of the need) have complete sufficiency in everything being completely self-sufficient in Him and have an abundance for every good work and act of charity.

We know at the end of the day; we must activate and unlock wealth within us for the advancement of the Kingdom of God. God is so willingly to bless you beyond what you even think. We have been conditioned to believe that wealth and prosperity is not for us. This is error and not of God. God wants you to believe Him and yourself. He said in His word that He is able to make all grace (earthly blessing) come to you in abundance. You will have such an overflow for you to do the work of the Lord, do act of charity and have more than enough for you and I know that God will give you the blueprint to multiply as he did with the servant that had the 5 talents, he doubled it!

Remember, you must change your mindset, that you attract wealth, and you must believe God and believe that wealth is for you.

Prayer:

Father, I pray and declare Mark 9:23, that if thou canst believe, all things are possible to Him that believeth. I thank you that your intercessors believe that wealth and prosperity is for them, and it has been ordained since the foundation of the earth. Father, I thank you that you have removed every demonic cycle from their lives and their minds and souls have been delivered from the kingdom darkness. I break and destroy rejection, witchcraft and control in Jesus Name, I lose the liberty of the Lord upon your intercessors even now in the name of Jesus, amen

www.ingramcontent.com/pod-product-compliance
Lightning Source LLC
Chambersburg PA
CBHW070937120626
46546CB00004B/1444